© 2000 by Running Press
All rights reserved under the Pan-American
and International Copyright Conventions
Printed in the United States

9 8 7 6 5 4
Digit on the right indicates the number of this printing

Library of Congress Cataloging-in-Publication Number 99-075158

ISBN 0-7624-0399-3

Picture research by Susan Oyama
Cover and interior design by Bryn Ashburn
Edited by Patty Aitken Smith
Typography: americana, coronet, futura

This book may be ordered by mail from the publisher.
Please include $2.50 for postage and handling.
But try your bookstore first!

Running Press Book Publishers
125 South Twenty-second Street
Philadelphia, Pennsylvania 19103-4399

Visit us on the web!
www.runningpress.com

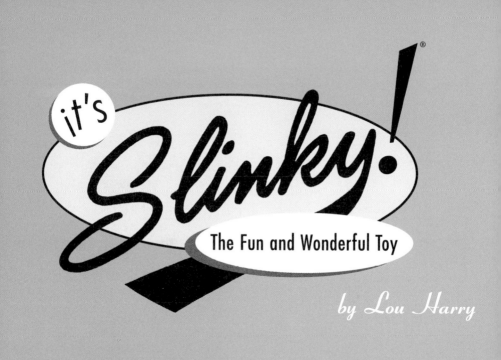

it's **Slinky!**

The Fun and Wonderful Toy

by Lou Harry

RUNNING PRESS
PHILADELPHIA · LONDON

This book is dedicated to Betty James, mother of the Slinky®. And to the memory of Adolf "Budd" Kalafski, a Wildwood, New Jersey, boardwalk entrepreneur who taught this book's writer the fun in business and the business of fun.

CONTENTS

Slinky®

Aptitude Test (SAT)

True or False

1. Slinky® is produced in mainland China.
2. The Slinky® was first sold in Gimbels department store in Philadelphia.
3. The Slinky® was first called the Quirly.
4. A single standard-sized Slinky® is 80 feet of metal coil.
5. The safety tips were added to the Slinky® in 1973.
6. In 1963, the Monkees sang the classic Slinky® commercial jingle in a public appearance.
7. Slinky® was used as an antenna in the jungle in the Vietnam war.
8. Slinky® Sillys are eyeglasses with Slinky® lenses.
9. Slinky® was used as a prop in Tom Hanks's movie, *Big*.
10. In the movie *Toy Story*, the Slinky Dog® was named Spot.

Answers on page 75.

Introduction

E very year a new group of kids falls
in love with this marvelous thing
that everyone knows as Slinky®.

Firmly entrenched among the elite of toydom,
Slinky® is spoken of in the same breath as such leg-
endary playthings as Barbie, G.I. Joe, Lincoln Logs,
Legos, Etch-a-Sketch, Frisbee, Tonka Trucks, and
Mr. Potato Head.

Yet even among this distinguished group, Slinky®
stands out. Poetic in its simplicity, beguiling in its vari-
ety, the Slinky® is almost magical in its ability to capture
the attention of children and adults and even more

magical in its ability to hold that attention. Generations of kids have watched Slinky® end-over-end down staircases. Generations of parents have stuffed stocking with them, handed them over as pick-me-ups to sick children, and tried gamely to untangle them (It's really not that hard to do, once you get the hang of it).

For decades, would-be entrepreneurs and toy executives have muttered "Why didn't I think of that?" as over 250 million were sold—enough for every person in the United States to have one.

"Nothing to Wind Up," announced the box. "Nothing to wear out." But that wasn't the half of it. Slinky® not only was and remains a great toy, it's also a great equalizer. When Slinky® first went on the market, it sold for $1. If that were adjusted for inflation, a Slinky® today would cost, well, a lot more than the standard

$1.99 that it sells for, more than half a century later (compare that to the increase in the cost of a movie ticket!). As such, it is one of the most affordable mass-produced toys in the world—one that rich and poor can find equally enjoyable.

As much as we want you to turn the page and read more about Slinky®, though, we understand that first you'll want to open up this new, limited edition Slinky® and play with it for a while.

Go on. Find a staircase and give Slinky® a tip from the top. Then take both ends and bounce it from hand to hand. Find a friend, and see how long you can stretch it.

Then come back to the book, which is not just a history of the Slinky®, it's also a celebration of it. In this volume, you'll not only find out about the amazing metal coil, but you'll also be reminded of the Slinky® jingle, learn about the science of Slinky® and read previously untold stories of the Slinky®.

Yes, everyone knows it's Slinky®.

But there's a lot you don't know about it.

Enjoy!

Slinky

Operating Instructions

1. TO WALK SLINKY® DOWN STAIRS

Place Slinky® on top stair. Grip coil at top and flip it over toward middle of the next lower step, releasing hold on Slinky®. Now Slinky® takes over and walks downstairs all by itself.

2. TO PLAY WITH SLINKY® IN HANDS

Hold end coils of Slinky® with both hands. Now raise and lower each hand in a rhythmic motion.

3. TO WALK SLINKY® DOWN INCLINE OR SLOPE

Any board or table top with a non-slip surface will do. Slope surface so rise equals about 1 foot for every 4 foot length. Place Slinky® at top, flip and watch Slinky® start down, end over end.

4. TO BOUNCE SLINKY® UP AND DOWN

Hold a few coils tightly in one hand, allowing rest of Slinky® to hang down. Now in a bouncing motion, move hand slowly up and down.

CAUTION

Do not use in moving vehicle. Do not throw coils out any window. Keep Slinky® away from face and eyes.

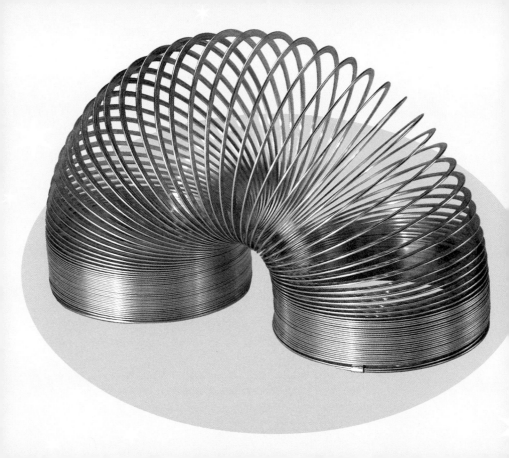

In the Beginning was the coil *

Not since Sir Isaac Newton was hit on the head with an apple has . . .

Okay, so that might be an exaggeration. But it was still, in hindsight, a pretty remarkable moment when Richard James, a $50-a-week marine engineer stationed at the Cramp shipyards in Philadelphia, observed a torsion spring fall off a table and roll around on the deck. (A torsion spring, by the way, is one with no compression or tension.)

Surely this was not the first torsion spring to have fallen and rolled around. And certainly other men at sea have seen such situations before.

Other men, though, probably ignored the escaped coil, or picked it up and put it back where it belonged.

Not Richard James.

He had that special something that separates ordinary folks from visionaries. He took the spring home to his wife, Betty, and utter those fateful words: "I think there could be a toy in this."

His wife agreed and, with a $500 loan, the couple ran tests, experimented with materials, and produced four hundred of the toys. What to call them? Betty James did some dictionary searching and came up with the perfect moniker—Slinky®.

But there was a problem. And to understand that problem you have to imagine yourself in a world that never knew what a Slinky® was or could do. Sure, it seems obvious now, but in 1945 a coiled spring on a store shelf looks like nothing more than a coiled spring on a store shelf.

So the Jameses took matters into their own hands.

On a stormy night in November, 1945, Richard and Betty James, through a special arrangement with Gimbels, the venerable center city Philadelphia retailer, were granted permission to set up an inclined plane in the toy department and demonstrate the spring's battery-less walking abilities.

Betty was prepared for the worst. She had planned on bringing a friend along and, if business was slow, the pair would pretend to be customers, gushing enthusiastically in an attempt to draw attention to the table.

WALKS

Slinky

DOWN

FAMOUS WALKING SPRING TOY

STAIRS

But as it turned out, such faking was not necessary. Betty and her pal arrived and saw a mob of people surrounding the Slinky® stand. Within an hour and a half, the Jameses were sold out of their creation.

A toy was born.

Richard and Betty James had no experience running a company—they just knew they had a great idea.

So did the general public. As word spread, demand grew. Richard created Slinkys® as fast as he could while Betty wrapped each in yellow paper and took care of the bookkeeping. Boxes didn't come until later, when the Jameses began using distributors rather than delivering the products themselves.

The boxes made a big difference. At Macy's in New York City, for instance, they were so popular that the Jameses were called and told that Slinkys® had to be taken off the shelves because the crowd around them was creating a fire hazard.

"Oh, it was an exciting time," recalls Betty James. "We got a lot of publicity and all the magazine's wanted to know about Slinky®. Everyone was calling for them. We didn't have enough money to make great big orders so we had to make what we could afford and Richard would drive the delivery and I would take the invoice and get the money so that we had the next day's supply. We lived in an old farmhouse that had a long tunnel in the basement and I remember putting the money in a roasting pan and shoving it back in the tunnel so that if anyone got in they wouldn't find our money."

Soon, though, it was too much business for the duo to handle by themselves.

left: This advertisement shows the wonderful press that Slinky® received in 1949.
opposite: The site of the first Slinky® factory was opened in Philadelphia in 1945.

In 1948 they had built a factory for twenty employees in the suburban Philadelphia town, Clifton Heights, in Delaware County. In 1951, with sales still growing, they moved the plant to nearby Paoli.

As the company expanded, so did the product line. New Slinky® toys, including Slinky Jr.® and the Slinky Dog®, were developed while non-coiled toys such as building kits were added to the inventory. However, Slinky® remained the core product of James Industries.

opposite: The James family opened the Paoli plant with a ribbon-cutting ceremony in 1951.

But—it wasn't always easy getting the steel needed for the creation of Slinkys®.

Once Richard James was taken ill during a steel strike and the materials just weren't coming in.

In what she describes as a clear case of fools rushing in where angels fear to tread, Betty James called the President of Pittsburgh Steel and told him that she was sure he wouldn't have gotten where he was if he didn't have compassion and empathy for people.

She said she had to have steel or the company would go bankrupt.

He sent the steel.

"For what shall it profit a man, if he gain the whole world, and suffer the loss of his soul." MARK 8:36
(Search the Scriptures)

ORIGINAL SLINKY $1.00

SLINKY SOLDIERS $2.00

SLINKY SEAL $1.00

SLINKY HANDCAR $2.00

SLINKY SPIRAL $1.00

SLINKY DOG $2.00

Insist on

Slinky® Toys

AT YOUR NEAREST TOY COUNTER

JAMES INDUSTRIES, PAOLI, PA.

SLINKY WORM • SLINKY TRAIN • SLINKY JUNIOR • SLINKY EYES • SLINKY BUCKO

How a Slinky® Is Made

Sorry, but that's a secret.

Well, maybe not all of it. What can be said is that giant coils of steel are loaded onto the original machines designed and engineered by Richard James in 1945. As the wire comes off its core, it is spun into a coil by a specially-created machine and cut at the 80-foot mark. A worker attaches the metal safety tips and places the Slinky® on a conveyor belt. In about nine to eleven seconds, a Slinky® has been birthed. It's still very close to the same product that was sold that fateful night at Gimbels department store, with a few minor differences. The earliest Slinkys® were made of an expensive blue-black Swedish steel. The company soon switched to a more silver steel. In the mid-1960s Slinky® was coated, and the color was made even more silvery. In 1973, the metal tips were put on the ends of the Slinky®. It may sound simple, but if it were, then why don't the imitation Slinkys® that periodically find their way onto the market have the durability and springiness of the original?

The truth is: Nobody does it better than James Industries.

opposite: This early Slinky® is made of blue-black Swedish

Slinky *Almost Misses a Step*

etty James had risen to the challenge of running a growing company, and luckily had the strength and fortitude to see her through the terrible difficulties that she was about to face.

Inexplicably, Richard James was not satisfied with developing one of the most popular toys in history and began a personal search for something more.

In the mid-1950s, he began to show an interest in religion, and, according to Betty James, started neglecting the company.

"He was giving some machinery away and we had to have the attorney stop it," she says. "I'm still not really sure what the religion was, but by about 1959 he was heavily involved and said he was going to work building printing presses for a Bible publisher." In 1960 he left. In 1974, he died in South America.

Fortunately, Betty James had suspected that things were going seriously awry.

"I was afraid that he would give his stock away and that I wouldn't be able to keep going," she explains. "So I went to the attorney and asked how I could get the stock into the children's names—except two shares to me which would make me the majority shareholder. He said that I'd have to get Richard to sign to it. I said fine. I knew him well enough to know that when he was in a hurry, he wouldn't read anything. So I waited until he got real busy and said, 'the attorney sent this over, will you sign it?' He did, and that's how the kids got it."

"I've always been crafty," she adds.

After her husband left, Betty James realized that she needed to stabilize life for her six children. She bought a home in Hollidaysburg, a small town near Altoona in central Pennsylvania where she had relatives who

opposite: Betty James on the factory floor of the Hollidaysburg plant in 1965.

could help them. Then, she rented a factory to make Slinky® and moved the whole operation there. She began to tackle the stack of bills left by her husband and learn the nuts and bolts of the business.

Four years later—after some very rocky times—James Industries started to make money again. With the assistance of the people of Hollidaysburg—who helped her relocate the company and build a new factory—she turned the company around. All the while, Betty James resisted a buy-out, turning down offers from large toy conglomerates on a regular basis.

In 1998, Betty James—whose Cadillac sports a license plate that reads SLINKY—finally was ready for retirement and found a company that she could com-fortably turn her baby over to. She sold James Industries to Poof Products, a Michigan-based company that also believes in supporting the American economy by manufacturing Slinky® in the United States.

After fifty-three years of running James Industries, Betty James is now retired with six children and sixteen grandchildren. She still lives in Hollidaysburg.

33 USA

Slinky Craze Begins 1945

1990

Slinky® Stamp

Slinky® was chosen as one of fifteen stamps to represent the 1940s in the Celebrate the Century collection of stamps from the U.S. Postal Service. A retired Betty James celebrated the release of the Slinky® stamp on February 18, 1999, at the company headquarters in Hollidaysburg, PA.

above: The Slinky® stamp commemorating the 1940s.
opposite: Betty James at the celebration of the release of the stamp and an advertisement thanking consumers for fifty wonderful years.

3
USA

Craze Begins 1945

1999

Slinky

ORIGINAL
Slinky

ORIGINAL
Slinky

1945

1995

Once in a lifetime...
THANK YOU!
FOR 50 WONDERFUL YEARS

JAMES INDUSTRIES, INC. • ROOM 608 • 200 FIFTH AVENUE

Slinky

Imitators, Spin-offs, and Specialty Slinkys®

Over the years, there were attempts to cash in on the Slinky® phenomenon almost from the beginning. Even the company that James Industries licensed to make Slinky® one day turned around and said they were going to make their own.

They called it Quirly, but a court case involving patent law went in favor of James Industries and the Quirly disappeared from the market.

Even now, low budget coiled-wire toys can be found on the market. But none can match the staying power—or the playing power—of the Slinky®.

brass

gold

collector's edition

The core of Slinky's® popularity has always been the simple metal coil toy. Yet there's been a massive menagerie of official Slinky® spin-offs and variations on that simple, original toy. Some have obviously been more successful than others.

In addition to the standard Slinky®, James Industries manufactures a line of specialty Slinkys® including one made of solid brass that comes in a felt-finish box, a gold plated Slinky® in a wooden box and a collector's edition Slinky® packaged in a box featuring the original design.

Then there's Slinky Jr.®, which is easy to fit in a pocket.

Betty and Richard James were concerned about introducing the shrunken version of the original into the market. The problem? What happens if consumers fall in love with the miniature version and ignore the original?

It turns out there was need to worry. Both endured.

Some purists wanted to have no part of Plastic Slinky®, Plastic Slinky Jr.®, Neon Slinky®, and Neon Slinky Jr.® But purists are but a small part of the toy market. The plastic Slinky® with its slightly different acoustics and bright colors and the Slinky® Extreme which is a standard Slinky® covered in bright fabric have both sold well and keep the toy fresh in the marketplace.

Slinky® spin-offs have surged since Helen Malsed came to James Industries with an idea for a new product.

The prototype that she presented was of a toy she had conceived as a modification of a Slinky® that her son had received as a Christmas gift.

"She immediately made my dad go down in the basement, take apart one of my other toys and put the wheels on the Slinky®," recounts her son."That was the beginning of the Slinky® Train."

"We thought it was a great idea," recalls Betty James of the rolling version of her hit toy, "and we told her that if she got a patent on it, we would pay her royalties."

Malsed did, and James Industries lived up to their end of the bargain. Slinky® suddenly didn't have to be tipped from the top of a staircase to be mobile.

Malsed also invented the Slinky Dog®, which begot the Slinky Dog, Jr.® and the soft-bodied Slinky® Plus Dog. The friendly pup had a major resurgence in popularity when he played a pivotal role in the computer-animated movie *Toy Story* and its sequel, *Toy Story 2*.

Canines weren't the only Slinky® animals, though. Other spin-offs included the Slinky Seal®, the Slinky Worm®, the Slinky Hippopotamus® and the Slinky Frog®.

Then there is Slinky® Pets, a line of animals with felt-covered Slinky® bodies and plush faces and tails. One of the latest Slinky® products, it has already proven itself to be a huge hit. So far, the playful beasts have included frogs, giraffes, sheep, tigers, pigs and many others.

Slinky® technology has been applied to everything from Slinky® Crazy Eyes—a pair of glasses with pop-out eyeballs—to Slinky® Sillys, wacky characters with Slinky® arms and legs (for added fun, the feet and hands stick to windows and mirrors).

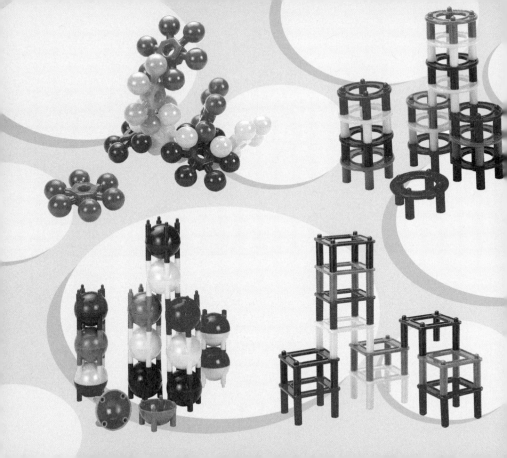

And James Industries has attached the Slinky® name to more than just coiled-wire products. They also create Slinky® Spinwheels (available in holographic, metallic, and stars and stripes varieties), Dabblin' Dough (Slinky's® version of kid-friendly modeling clay), Form-a-Tions, Triangles, Tower-ifics, Ringa-Majigs, Ji-Gan-Tiks and Moli-Q's (all stacking and building toys that each offer new ways to create towering structures), cheerleading batons and Miss America pompons.

And that's not all. There's also Slinky® Pik-Up Stiks (a color-coded variation on the classic kids' game) and Slinky® Pop Toobs (bendable, snappable noise-making tubes) as well as a pair of attempts to translate Slinky's® popularity into the board game market. There was Slink 'Em, a 1947 game based on a Slinky®, and The Amazing Slinky® Game, a later board game

with a slogan on the box that reads "For fun it's a wonderful game!" Both board games are now much-coveted collectors' items.

Not everything that came out of the James Industries' factories was a success though. Like any company, there were a few bloopers along the way.

"Oh, we had some really lousy ones," admits Betty James. "There were a lot of things that didn't work. One was Giant Jacks. They looked great. They did not sell. We had a lot of Giant Jacks. Then we had another item that was made out of sponge. They were different characters, and you put them in water and they would swell up. It flopped, but boy did we have sponge. Then we had another thing that had figures made out of foam in a frame. It had little knobs on it and they would make the figures wiggle. But the knobs should have been on the front so you could see it. It went down the tubes."

Oh well, you can't win them all.

There are thousands of ways to play with a Slinky®.
That's been proven by generation after generation of creative kids,
curious adults and toymakers looking for Slinky® variations. But, while intended
as a toy, Slinky® has been put to many other uses.

Nearly since its creation, inventors have taken the Slinky® and tried to bend it to
their creative wills. One southerner with an agricultural problem approached James
Industries with plans for a Slinky®-using pecan-picking contraption. Permission was granted
and pecans have been picked with the help of a Slinky® ever since.

Others have approached—and been granted—permission by James Industries to use
the Slinky® in drapery holders, curtains, light fixtures, window decorations, gutter protectors,
pigeon repellers, bird house protectors and mail holders. During the Vietnam War,
U.S. soldiers even threw Slinkys® into trees to act as makeshift radio antennas.

But perhaps the most worthwhile alternative use for Slinky®
has been as a therapeutic tool for people with strokes
and other disorders. See: not only is Slinky®
fun to play with, it's patriotic
and healthy, too.

It's Slinky®

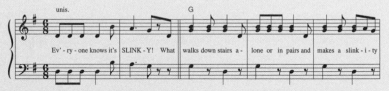

Slinky® Enters

Pop Culture

he Slinky® has been continuously airing on television longer than any other commercial in the country. *It's Slinky!*® is the stuff of jingle legend.

With music and lyrics by Homer Festperman and Charles Weagley, the song first hit the airwaves in 1962. The idea was to set a song to the sound of a Slinky® walking down stairs and the actual sound of a Slinky® was included in the original commercial.

It came from an ad agency in Columbia, South Carolina, which originally commissioned it for use by a regional wholesaler. When the James Industries

folks heard it, though, they loved it so much that they bought it outright, even though Betty James says she never actually met the men who wrote it.

Every now and then the music was updated to accommodate the latest musical trends—more guitar sometimes, other times more brass.

In 1984 it was selected for a television special on great TV commercials hosted by Ed McMahon for Johnny Carson Productions. It's also one of fifty tunes on the Tee Vee Tunes; The Commercials CD from TVT Records, where it is enshrined in the company of *If You Like Fluff, Fluff, Fluff* (for Fluffernutter), *I'm A Chiquita Banana, Plop, Plop, Fizz, Fizz* (the Alka-Seltzer song), and *My Dog's Better Than Your Dog* (for Ken-L Ration dog food). Interestingly, it's the only toy song that made

it onto the disc (unless you count the little prize in the Cracker Jack box as a real toy).

Recently, American Isuzu Motors asked James Industries if they could use the classic Slinky® jingle for their car ads on TV. Toy music in a car commercial? Surely the Madison Avenue folks knew what they were doing.

A deal was worked out, and soon commercials were on the air for the Amigo, a sport-utility vehicle. Featuring retro-coiffed passengers decked out in '70s garb, the ad modified the tune to sell the car—which even drove down stairs to mock the familiar "What walks down stairs" lyric (changed to "What goes down stairs").

But apparently it didn't quite do its job. The spots were pulled after only two months on the air.

Commercials were just the beginning of Slinky's® appearance on television. Back in the days of black and white TV, when James Industries ran a Slinky® commercial during the local kids show, the host of the show would sometimes ad-lib play with a Slinky® upon return from commercial break. As a reward for supporting their respective shows, *Captain Delta* and *Captain Satellite* often had Slinky® appear on their shows. Recently, the Slinky® has appeared in primetime sitcoms like *The Drew Carey Show*, *Happy Days*, and *Wings* as well as dramas like *Law and Order* and *St. Elsewhere*. Slinky® has also been featured on an episode of the sci-fi series *The Pretender*.

Slinky® has been able to successfully make the jump from television to the big screen.

Although never earning an Oscar, the coiled one has made star-making cameos in such films as *Other People's Money* with Danny DeVito, *Demolition Man* with Sylvester Stallone, *Hairspray* with Ricki Lake, and *Ace Ventura: When Nature Calls*, with Jim Carrey. It has even foreshadowed seismic disturbances in *Volcano*. It was a key part of the inner workings of *Inspector Gadget*.

Without a question, though, the highlight of Slinky's® film career has been *Toy Story*. Here, not only was the Slinky Dog® a featured character, he was also given the name Slinky®—Slink to his friends.

Throughout the film, this heroic pooch shows a wide range of emotions, performs acts of extreme heroism, and even proves an adept checkers player.

Jim Varney, best known for his movie and TV appearances as the character Ernest, was the voice of Slinky® in *Toy Story*. His performance helped revive the Slinky Dog® as a key component in the James Industries catalog.

When the producers originally contacted Betty James, though, she thought it was a joke. "When they said it was this Disney office," she remembers, "I said 'Yeah, and I'm Minnie Mouse.'"

After the movie was released, Disney asked if Betty James had any of the original dogs. She sent

above: The original Slinky Dog®.
opposite: Slinky Dog® in Disney's *Toy Story*.

two, which were used in displays at Disney World in Florida and Disneyland in California.

Slinky's® fame is not limited to the realm of the film world—it has also achieved a level of fame in print media. Besides being the subject for articles in such popular magazines as *Forbes*, *Reader's Digest*, *Cosmopolitan*, *Redbook*, the *New York Times Magazine*, *Time* and more, it has been featured in several syndicated comic strips such as *Mother Goose* and *Grimm*, *Family Circus*, *Rose Is Rose*, *Calvin and Hobbes*, and *B.C.* (three times).

Finally, the Slinky® has truly made its way into every level of our cultural consciousness—from the lowest to the highest—with its exhibition at both the Metropolitan Museum of Art and the Smithsonian Institution.

above: The fun of Slinky® is immortalized in this *B.C.* comic strip by Johnny Hart which ran on November 25, 1980.

The Ultimate Slinky®

"The average Slinky® is fine for walking down steps, but I want
to send waves!" declared Robin Whittle of Melbourne, Australia. And he meant it.
He called his creation Sliiiiiiiiiiiiiiiiiinky, and his work is something to behold. In a unique
combination of art, science, and chutzpah, the intrepid Aussie soldered together
33 ½ Slinkys®, combined them with 418 fine elastic supports and hung the contraption
on a frame of aluminum tubing. He's used the result to test wave theory,
to explore sound waves, and to have a plain old good time.
"Whether people consider this art or not, I don't mind," he said,
"I see a lot of art in many everyday things people do."

opposite: Sliiiiiiiiiiiiiiiiiinky by Robin Whittle of Melbourne, Australia.

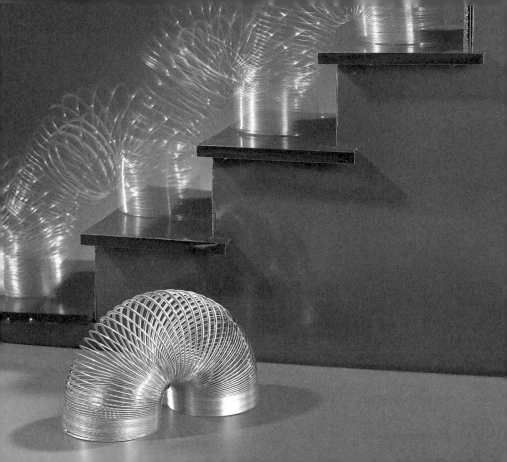

The Science of Slinky®

L ike any subject, science can be made interesting
or dull, depending on the teacher in front of the
room. Throughout the years, savvy teachers
with an understanding of how play can lead to understanding have used Slinky® to explore some basic—
and some not-so-basic—scientific principles. Using a
common Slinky®, for instance, one can begin to grasp
the differences between potential and kinetic energy

   Taken out of the box and stood on one circular end,
the Slinky® is the very picture of stored, or potential,
energy. Since an object at rest tends to stay at rest,

opposite: Slinky® demonstrates potential energy and kinetic energy.

according to scientific law, then nothing much is going on when the Slinky® is in this potential energy state. That lack of movement is also called inertia.

Now, at the top of a staircase, tip one end over the other into an arc and let go, then you are dealing with kinetic energy. A complex exchange begins as each ring of the Slinky® is pulled, initially by gravity, alternating from potential to kinetic energy.

What's going on here? Well, as the Slinky® takes its walk, energy is transferred along in a longitudinal wave. That's a wave in which the vibration is in the same direction as that in which the wave is traveling, as in sound waves. The speed of the Slinky® depends on the tension in the spring, the metal's mass, the diameter of the coils and the height of each step.

But step walking isn't the only way that scientific ideas are illustrated by Slinky®.

Centripetal force is demonstrated when a Slinky® is whirled around one's head (with nothing breakable or human nearby). Your hand needs to supply force to keep it from flying off in the straight line it wants to go. The faster you make the Slinky® spin, the more difficult it is to hold on to and, thus, the more force your hand needs to exert to keep the Slinky® from flying away. Objects in motion tend to want to stay in motion in a straight line, which is why the Slinky® stays extended and pulls this way.

Want a basic understanding of atmospheric pressure? Hold a Slinky® at about eye-level and let one end fall. Notice how the coils are not separated by the same amount of space. In fact, the coils nearest to the ground are closest together. The ones by your hand are farthest apart. The coils at the bottom have the most weight on top of them. The ones at the top have the least. The lower altitudes are represented by the bottom coils where atmospheric pressure is greatest.

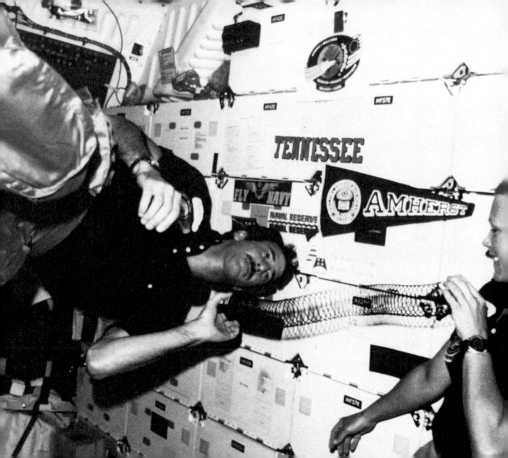

Scientists use Slinkys® to model ocean waves, seismic waves and rotational waves as well as antennas for receiving radio waves.

Slinky® science is popular on the world wide web. At one site, Slinky® is used to supplement a PBS science program *Newton's Apple*. They have a page on Slinky® Physics that includes discussion topics ("Why can't a Slinky® go upstairs?") and suggested activities. It's a good site (www.ktca.org/newtons/9/slink.html) for teachers to visit before working Slinky® into their curriculum.

Want to see NASA astronauts in space testing the power of Slinky® in zero gravity? See Space Shuttle Discovery astronauts playing with it on the NASA website.

opposite: NASA astronauts use Slinky® in experiments on a space shuttle.

A Lot of Wire

Over 3,030,000 miles of wire (or 50,000 tons) have been used in Slinkys® since the toy was created— enough wire to encircle the Earth 126 times. That's more wire than has been strung by all North American telephone companies combined.

In Conclusion

And so now it comes down to the wire.

Think of this as the print equivalent of that climactic moment when the Slinky® at last arrives at the bottom of the steps. In the time it's taken you to read this book (assuming you've devoured it without stopping to play with the Slinky® or otherwise go on with your life), about 500 freshly minted Slinkys® have been brought into the world from the Hollidaysburg plant. That's 500 lengths of metal turned into 500 toys in the same way that the process has been carried out for years.

Visiting the place where that happens—the Slinky® plant in Hollidaysburg (sorry, but it's not open to the public, although you can visit the really neat gift shop)—one can't help being overcome by the result of that one simple shipboard epiphany. Here, the sheer quantity of coils is overwhelming. It's impossible not to think of how that initial spring has managed somehow to twist and turn its way through the better part of a century only to arrive at a point where it has wound up on a stamp, appeared in movies, and achieved a pop cultural position as one of the most recognizable objects in the world. That such simplicity can have such lasting value is perhaps where the ultimate lesson of the Slinky® lies. "You don't have to be smart, athletic, rich or clever to appreciate the Slinky®," said a *Reader's Digest* scribe, "It's a toy for regular people. You pick it up and instinctively know to part those coils into two halves and rock the Slinky® back and forth." Indeed, there's something instinctual about playing with a Slinky®. Sure, it has helped teach scientific principles, encouraged one man to create a legendary screen character, obsessed an Aussie into creating a mammoth work of art. Yet none of these additional uses has gotten in the way of the Slinky's® primary function—fun.

That and that alone is the reason for its endurance. That's why we love it. Don't be surprised if your grandchildren and their grandchildren are still playing with the fun and wonderful Slinky®.

- When your world gets twisted,
a little patience will help work things out.
- It's possible to go around in circles and still end up
pretty close to where you started.
- It's one thing to be popular, but classic transcends trends.
- Never underestimate the power of a catchy tune.
- Simplicity can be magical—and fun.
- Science is interesting if you have the right tools.
- Some things are great in and of themselves.
They don't need accessories.
- Be original and success will follow.

Slinky

Aptitude Test (SAT)

Answers

1. False. The Slinky® has always been manufactured in America, first in the Philadelphia area, then in central Pennsylvania.
2. True.
3. False. The Slinky® was always called the Slinky®. The Quirly was an early attempt to copy the Slinky®.
4. True.
5. True.
6. False.
7. True.
8. False. Slinky® Sillies are characters with Slinky®s for arms and legs.
9. False. However Slinky® has been featured in many other movies such as *Other People's Money*, one of the toy's many movie appearances.
10. False. It's a trick question: He was simply called Slinky®.

About the *Author*

Lou Harry, writing as Voodoo Lou, is the author of *The Voodoo Kit* and *The Office Voodoo Kit*. As himself, he has written the book *Strange Philadelphia* and contributed to more than three dozen publications including *POV*, *Art and Antiques*, and *Children's Digest*. He is a senior editor of *Indianapolis Monthly* and lives in Indiana with his wife and their three Slinky®-loving children.

"It's self-contained, easy to manufacture, inexpensive to buy... Best of all, Slinky® is still endlessly fascinating to children and adults alike."

—Gil Asakawa and Leland Rucker, authors of *The Toy Book*

"But for one small bump, we might have missed out on the pleasures of this hard-to-classify piece of magic... and design classic."

—*Lands End* catalog